BY HIS STRIPES
YOU ARE HEALED!

BY:

JOHN CHRISTY

AjON MULTIMEDIA
"The Word is Eternal" Isaiah 40:8

Printed in the United States of America

Published by Aion Multimedia
20118 N 67th Ave
Suite 300-446
Glendale AZ 85308
www.aionmultimedia.com

ISBN-13: 978-0-9976046-1-0

TABLE OF CONTENTS

Foreword

You have made it past the cover, the title of the book has gotten your attention and now your reading the foreword. So, I'll keep this short. What caught your interest/attention? Do you need a physical healing from an addiction, disease, sickness, illness, emotional relationships, diagnosis...? This is the book for you. It is Holy Spirit led, based strictly and solely on The Word of God. This book shows you what Scripture says about being healed. It's intended to open your eyes and heart and clear up any questions you might have. I invite you to read on and see for yourself what The Word of God says about healing and being healed. The only folk Jesus did not heal were the ones who did not seek HIM out! God bless you, and enjoy HIS presence while reading and discovering healing truths.

Acknowledgements

I'd like to thank several people who helped to make this dream come true. My wife Denise and our children Johnny, Hannah, and James; those of you who contributed financially to the publication of the book and those of you who certainly supported me through prayer. I am forever blessed by your love friendship and support. The blessings of the Lord do maketh rich. God bless you all and I love each and every one of you. Phil.4:13

Introduction

Healed – *cause a wound, injury, or person to become sound or healthy again.*

Synonyms: make better, make well, cure, treat, restore to health, recover, mend, improve.

Matthew 9:35 *"Jesus went through all the towns and villages, teaching in their synagogues, preaching the good news of the kingdom and healing every disease and sickness."*

Isaiah 53:4-6 *"Surely HE took up our infirmities and carried our sorrows, yet we considered HIM stricken by God, smitten by HIM, and afflicted. But HE was pierced for our transgressions, HE was crushed for our iniquities; the punishment that brought us peace was upon HIM, and by HIS wounds we are healed. We all, like sheep, have gone astray, each of us has turned to his own way; and the Lord has laid on HIM the iniquity of us all."*

1 Peter 2:24b *"by HIS wounds you have been healed."*

Why have you picked up this book? Is there something about the Bible and healing that you wonder about? Do you or someone close to you, a family member, a friend, or yourself need healing? Do you know someone that has been diagnosed with a serious or terminally ill physical attack, a sickness or disease? Is it God's will NOT to heal? Would God inflict you with a disease, illness or sickness to try and teach you something?

The hope of this book is to show you (or that special someone) what Scriptures, the Word of God (The Bible) says about healing and being healed. This is not an accident that you have picked up this book. It is not by "luck" or "happenstance" but by guidance and direction of the Holy Spirit! It is intended to open your eyes to healing today, and clear up any questions you might have on healing and what the Word of God says about healing and that you, too, (or that special someone) can be and are healed, in the mighty, powerful, healing, supplying, wonderful, providing, and awesome name of Jesus Christ!

Even though I have been healed on five serious occasions, witnessed folks receiving their healing, been a part of people being healed, read and heard testimonies on folk getting and receiving their healing, this book is strictly about what the Holy Bible, the Word of God, has to say about healing. I have NEVER NOT been healed (and as of September 30, 2015, I turned 60 years young), but none of my testimonies, nothing from any commentaries, or other folk's healing will you find in this book. This text is just straight from God's Word. What better source is there than HIS Word! 2 Timothy 3:16-17 says, "All Scripture is God breathed and is useful for teaching, rebuking, correcting, and training in righteousness, so that then man [and woman] of God may be thoroughly equipped for every good work." The Holy Spirit has guided and directed me as to what to put in this book for your encouragement, to receive your healing and to know that healing is for today — for us, for you and for me! I invite you to read and see for yourself what the Bible says about healing. I've gotten mine, and now it is time for you to get yours! God's Word in our mouths has the same power and authority as HIS

Word in HIS mouth! God bless you and enJOY! Read on and receive your healing now, today in Jesus' name! Amen!

I have so felt compelled by the Holy Spirit to write a book on healing of our physical bodies and what the Word of God says about healing. Funny thing, there has already been a very good book written about healing called *The Holy Bible*— a bestseller! Interestingly enough, people are still trying to write about healing, explain it, claim that it is not always God's will to heal (poppycock to that!) understand it, figure out how it works, wrap their minds around it, find a key/pattern to it, and even say it doesn't always work, didn't work…etc. But I am here to tell you and allow you to read my book that will convince you that healing is for real; healing is for today. Healing did not cease when Jesus died (remember HE died physically but is alive today spiritually!) but is for us today. When someone says, "It is NOT always God's will to heal," I respond to that by saying, "Show me in *The Holy Bible*, the Word of God, where you find that statement!" You can't and you won't because it is not found anywhere in the Bible! The only folk Jesus did not heal were the folk who did not seek HIM out! 2 Timothy 3:16-17 says that "all Scripture is God-breathed and is useful in teaching, rebuking, correcting and training in righteousness, so that the servant of God may be thoroughly equipped for every good work."

The Word of God is Truth:

Proverbs 3:5 *"Trust in the Lord with all your heart and lean not on your own understanding;"*

John 17:17 *"Sanctify them by Truth; Your Word is Truth."*

John 8:32 *"Then you will know the Truth, and the Truth will set you free."*

Numbers 23:19 *"God is not human, that HE should lie, not a human being, that HE should change HIS mind. Does HE speak and then not act? Does HE promise and not fulfill?*

Isaiah 55:8-9,11 *" 'For MY thoughts are not your thoughts, neither are your ways MY ways,' declares The Lord. 'As The Heavens are higher than the Earth, so are MY ways higher than your ways and MY thoughts than your thoughts... So is MY Word that goes out of MY mouth: It will not return to ME empty, but will accomplish what I desire and achieve the purpose for which I sent it.' "*

Never judge whether or not the Word of God is right based on what happened to someone else or what even happened to you based on what you thought/wanted or even prayed to happen.

The enemy is a liar:

John 8:44 *"You belong to your father, the devil, and you want to carry out your father's desires. He was a murderer from the beginning, not holding to the truth, for there is no truth in him. When he lies, he speaks his native language, for he is a liar and the father of lies."*

John 10:10 *"The thief comes only to steal, kill and destroy; I (Jesus speaking) have come that they may have life, and have it to the full."*

1 Peter 5:8 *"Be alert and of sober mind. Your enemy the devil prowls around like a roaring lion looking for someone to devour."*

But my friend, take heart, The Bible says in James 4:7-8a "Submit your selves, then, to God. Resist the devil, and he will flee from you. Come near to God and He will come near to you…" When you pray, and your prayers line up with the Word of God, you will have what you pray for! That is a spiritual law. Doubt, worry, discouragement, uncertainty, not being sure, thinking it may not happen, all are prayer killers. They destroy your prayers because you are, in a sense, doubting God and HIS Word and that is not good. James 1:6-7 "But when he asks, he must believe and not doubt, because he who doubts is like a wave of the sea. Blown and tossed by the wind. That man should not think he will receive anything from the Lord; he is a double-minded man, unstable in all he does." Mark 11:24-26, "Therefore I tell you, whatever you ask for in prayer, believe that you have received it, and it will be yours. And when you stand praying, if you hold anything against anyone, forgive him, so that your Father in Heaven may forgive you your sins." Matthew 21:21-22, "Jesus replied, 'I tell you the truth, if you have faith and do not doubt,…IF you believe, you will receive whatever you ask for in prayer." So, one must read the Word of God, study HIS Word, pray, and in many cases meet with a friend/prayer partner— someone who can help guide and direct you as to what the Word of God is saying— but who better than God and Jesus HIMSELF, and don't forget, the Holy Spirit. (Read all of John 14! Pay close attention to verses 16, 17 and 26.)

The Bible in the Gospels and The book of Acts clearly and specifically states the healing power of Jesus. The book of Matthew has the most accounts of Jesus' healing power, while The book of John records only four. Luke does record a healing miracle (the crippled woman healed on the sabbath) that none of the other three Gospel writers recorded. "Jesus did many other things as well. If every one of them were written down, I suppose that even the whole world would not have room for the books that would be written" (John 21:25). Based on that Scripture, we have just the tip of the iceberg of Jesus' healing and miracles. But nonetheless, Jesus healed folk then and HE is still healing folk today. Hebrews 13:8, "Jesus Christ is the same yesterday and today and forever." James 1:17, "Every good and perfect gift is from above, coming down from the Father of the Heavenly lights, who does not change like shifting shadows." Malachi 3:6a, "'I the Lord do not change.'"

So without further adieu, let's get into the meat of this book. Praise God!

By His Stripes, You Are Healed!

One very familiar and important Scripture on (and of) our healing that Jesus bought and paid for is Isaiah 53:4-5. "Surely HE took up our pain and bore our suffering, yet we considered HIM punished by God, stricken by HIM, and afflicted. But He was pierced for our transgressions, HE was crushed for out iniquities; the punishment that brought us peace was on HIM, and by HIS wounds we are healed." Look at what The Amplified Bible says;"But [in fact] HE has borne our griefs, and HE has carried our sorrows and pains; Yet we [ignorantly] assumed that HE was stricken, struck down by God and degraded and humiliated [by HIM]. But HE was wounded for our transgressions, HE was crushed for our wickedness [our sin, our injustice, our wrong doing]; the punishment [required] for our well-being fell on HIM, and by HIS stripes wounds) we are healed." 1 Peter 2:24 says, "'HE Himself bore our sins' in HIS body on the cross, so that we might die to sins and live for righteousness; 'by HIS wounds you have been healed.'" Notice the words used, "we ARE healed" and "you HAVE BEEN healed." Wow, that's good stuff and oh so true! It's a spiritual law. Now, one could or can argue and state their opinion; some of the most common "arguments" are, "I prayed for such-and-such's healing and he/she did not get healed…" "I trusted God and HIS Word and it didn't work." Say what you think it means,but one MUST believe in these two Scriptures as truth because they are true. Healing is for us today! We must have faith in HIS Word, we must have faith in GOD and HIS ability to preform HIS Word and trust HIM; HE bought and paid for it by the stripes HE bore on HIS back! Again, James 1:17 presents strong evidence of our healing (just like salvation is ours and belongs to us. Jesus' death on the cross sealed that when we come to HIM and repent of our sins and asked HIM into our lives). All we need to do is receive our healing, by HIS Grace through our faith! How simple is that? It is not difficult.

I believe that the enemy has lied to and ripped-off many of us who are in Christ of what belongs to us, including our healing, for many, many years. It is not only time to receive the truth, but start walking in the promise of what the Bible says about our healing TODAY! Throughout the decades, folk have prayed and sought "The Healing Power of Jesus" for friends, family, loved ones, themselves, and in many cases, healing did not take place. For those brothers and sisters, many came to the conclusion that since that person did not get, or receive, their healing, it must have been God's will NOT to heal them. NO WAY! The above pretty much disproves that statement, plus as I mentioned earlier, one will NEVER find in Scripture where that statement exists. Hosea 4:6a says, "MY people are destroyed from lack of knowledge." Sin, lack of faith in HIS Word, the five senses of human nature, our own minds, opinions, worry, doubt and other reasons inhibit our healing. So we blame God. Why? Based on what; physical outcomes or the Word of God? No, based on what happened, what the outcome was, what we thought would happen, a timeline, and it all did not work out the way we thought it would or should work out...So we conclude that it must have been God's will not to heal that person, that God does not heal everyone or it is not always God's will to heal everyone. That is so wrong and couldn't be farther from the truth of the Word of God!

Is salvation for everyone? Yes. Does everyone get saved? No. Does God want us to go to Hell? No. It breaks HIS heart for that to happen, yet it does happen.Folks do not accept Jesus as their Lord and Savior. Is healing for every one? Yes. Does everyone get healed? No. That, too, breaks HIS heart. 1 Timothy 2:4 says, "who wants all people to be saved and come to a knowledge of the truth." 2 Peter 3:9 says, "The Lord is not slow in keeping HIS promise, as some understand slowness. Instead HE is patient with you, not wanting anyone to perish, but everyone to come to repentance."

But it is NOT God's fault that not all are saved or healed.

2 Corinthians 5:15 *"And HE died for all, that those who live should no longer live for themselves but for HIM who died for them and was raised again."*

1 Peter 3:18 *"For Christ also suffered once for sins, the righteous for the unrighteous, to bring you to God. HE was put to death in the body but made alive in The Spirit. We all will die a physical death."*

Hebrews 9:27 *"Just as people are destined to die once, and after that to face judgement."*

But between now and that time, we are to be healthy, healed, and as Christ so that folk can see His love and His light in us.

9

Psalm 103:2-3 *"Praise the Lord, my soul, and forget not all his benefits— who forgives all your sins and heals all your diseases."*

2 Corinthians 5:20 says, "We are therefore Christ's ambassadors, as though God was making HIS appeal through us. We implore you on Christ's behalf: Be reconciled to God." Plus, healing just like salvation is ours; it belongs to us. Jesus bought and paid for them for us!

God spoke the world into existence (Genesis 1 says, "…and God said…") and there is power in our words.

Proverbs 18:21 *"Death and life are in the power of the tongue: and they that love it shall eat the fruit thereof."*

We must watch closely what we say out loud, what comes out of our mouth. Jesus cursed the fig tree and it dried from the roots up (Mark 11:12-25). We must learn to speak to our infirmity, cursing it as Jesus did the fig tree. We must learn to speak what The Word says about our healing. We must see ourselves healed. We must also be willing to receive our healing and be grateful and thankful for it. We must know what the Word of God says about our healing and speak it out loud, quoting Scripture —God's Word— to be healed. Declare it NOW, in Jesus' name. Receive your healing NOW, in Jesus' name. Thank HIM in advance for your healing; it is yours, it belongs to you. Stop allowing and letting the enemy rip you off from receiving what is yours, what belongs to you, in the mighty and powerful name of Jesus. Get busy and dive into the Word of God, see what the Word of God says about healing. Study, meditate, pray and seek God. As Matthew 6:33 says, "But seek first HIS Kingdom and HIS righteousness, and all these things will be given to you as well." When we give our lives to Jesus, surrendering everything to HIM, know and study HIS Word, knowing what The Word says about us and our healing, we then walk in HIS blessings and promises. Now let's look at, explore and study Scripture regarding healing. It's going to be fun and oh so rewarding!

When you study the Word of God and what it says about healing, you will need to look at some of the Greek and Hebrew words, their meanings/translations, and how they were translated into English. The Strong's Expanded Exhaustive Concordance of the Bible is a great source/ reference to have and I would strongly recommend you get one. For example, in Isaiah 53:4-5, verse 4 says, "surely HE has borne our griefs..." Here, "borne" in the Hebrew is "nasa" which means to lift up and remove away from. This will help you get a better understanding of what HIS Word is saying in that particular verse. It is, and will be, pretty awesome. Let me insist that every time you read and study the Word of God, before you do, pray. Ask God for knowledge, wisdom and understanding/clarity and thank HIM for revealing to you what HE is trying to get across to you through HIS Word. It works every time! Ask and seek God first and foremost in getting understanding of what HIS Word is saying. Going to other sources before God can cause confusion and misunderstanding. 1 Corinthians 14:33 says, "For God is not the author of confusion, but of peace..." Here is another example from Strong's Expanded Exhaustive Concordance: Isaiah 35:4b concludes, "HE will come and save you." When you look this up you find "Yasha" and its meaning "to open...to free, avenge, defend, deliver, help preserve, rescue...get victory. "Yeshuwah" means something saved; deliverance, and victory, prosperity, health, help, salvation, welfare. Now Jesus' name Yeshua means to save, rescue, preserve, and get victory. In Romans 10:9 at the end of this verse, we see the word "saved" which is Hebrew for "sozo"; to save, deliver, protect, heal, preserve, do well, be made whole(pretty cool, thank you Jesus). When we study healing in the Scriptures, we see pretty clearly that healing was not just what Jesus did during HIS 3-year ministry on Earth (as well as we see after HE was crucified in The book of Acts), but it is for today— for you, for HIS children, TODAY! John 14:12 says, "Very truly I tell you, whoever believes in ME will do what I have been doing. He will do greater things than these..." There are several Scriptures that deal with healing, most in the New Testament. I do wish to share five Old Testament Scriptures that address healing.

1. **Deuteronomy 28:7** "The Lord will grant that the enemies who rise up against you will be defeated before you. They will come at you from one direction but flee from you in seven."

2. **Isaiah 54:17** "'No weapon forged against you will prevail, and you will refute every tongue that accuses you. This is the heritage of the servants of The Lord, and this is their vindication from ME,' declares the Lord." In my opinion, I would have to say that "enemies" and "weapons" could be disease, sickness, a severe illness, a doctor's diagnosis, poor health, physical pain and are covered here under those terms.

3. **Deuteronomy 28:15, 21-22** "However, if you do not obey the Lord your God and do not carefully follow all HIS commands and decrees I am giving you today, all these curses will come on you and overtake you...The

Lord will plague you with diseases until HE has destroyed you from the land you are entering to possess. The Lord will strike you with wasting disease, fever and inflammation, with scorching heat and drought, with blight and mildew, which will plague you until you perish." Remember, this is Old Testament, and God sent HIS Son to die for us and to live in prosperity, healing and salvation New Testament.

4. **Deuteronomy 7:15** "The Lord will keep you free from every disease. HE will not inflict on you the horrible diseases you knew in Egypt, but HE will inflict them on all who hate you."

5. **1 Thessalonians 5:23** "May God Himself, the God of peace, sanctify you through and through. May your whole sprit, soul, and body be kept blameless at the coming of our Lord Jesus Christ." Look at what The Amplified Bible says, "Now may the God of peace Himself sanctify you through and through [that is, separate you from profane and vulgar things, make you pure and whole and undamaged—consecrated to HIM— set apart for HIS purpose]; and may your spirit and soul and body be kept complete and [be found] blameless at the coming of our Lord Jesus Christ."

When one is diagnosed with a terrible illness, disease, or physical attack, they have no peace. One feels terrible, frustrated, not good, restless, bothered, troubled, worried...etc. This provision is in the Old Testament under the Old Covenant to HIS children for us today! We are HIS children. Also, as mentioned before, Isaiah 53:4-5 certainly would be considered the chief or main

Old Testament Scripture and foundational healing Scripture.

>**Psalm 103:2-3** *"Praise the Lord, my soul, and forget not all HIS benefits—who forgives all your sins and heals all your diseases."*

In Jeremiah 1:12 we read, "The Lord said to me, 'You have seen correctly, for I am watching to see that MY Word is fulfilled.'" The Amplified Bible says "…watching over MY Word to fulfill it." Wow! Those are some powerful words! This sets the stage for what HIS Word says about healing and how HE performs it. James 1:22-25 says, "Do not merely listen to the Word, and so deceive your selves. Do what it says. Anyone who listens to the Word but does not do what it says is like someone who looks at his face in a mirror and, after looking at himself, goes away and immediately forgets what he looks like. But whoever looks intently into the perfect law that gives freedom, and continues in it—not forgetting what they have heard, but doing it—they will be blessed in what they do." Again, looking at James 1:17, it says, "Every good and perfect gift is from above, coming down from the Father of the heavenly lights, who does not change like shifting shadows." "Every good and perfect gift" and "blessed in what they do" pretty much negates disease, illness, sickness…because those ailments are not "good and perfect" and being sick is NOT a blessing! 1 John 5:14-15 states, "This is the confidence we have in approaching God: that if we ask anything according to HIS will, HE hears us. And if we know that HE hears us—whatever we ask--we know that we have what we asked of HIM." Simply put, God's will is HIS Word. So looking at HIS Word—and we know Romans 10:17 says, "So then Faith comes by hearing, and hearing by the Word of God"— knowing what HIS Word says, and having faith in HIS Word and hearing HIS Word, we are assured of our healing. It is a spiritual law (a statement of fact). Just like gravity is a natural law, so, too, is the Word of God. It is a spiritual law. It cannot be nullified, and it must always perform the way it was set up and said to perform. When we take a look at Isaiah 53:4-5 again, the King James Version (KJV) says, "and carried our sorrows," the Hebrew for "sorrows" is "mak'ob" and literally means "pain, to feel pain, to have pain, made sad, or sorrowful." So the physical pain or mental anguish Jesus took and carried, that is "sorrow." He borne our griefs, took away, lifted off, or removed them, by HIM taking the stripes and the beating. So why do we deal with stuff we have no business dealing with? The enemy is a liar and wants to take us out; he wants to destroy our testimony. When we pay attention to the physical— to the pain— we buy into his schemes, his lies and our focus is off Jesus and on the enemy. We must not forget 2 Corinthians 5:7 "For we walk by faith not by sight." That faith is having faith in what the Word says about us, our healing and what Jesus did and went through for us to have our healing, and be healed.

I want to draw your attention to a Scripture in Matthew 8:16-17 "When evening came, many who were demon-possessed were brought to HIM, and HE drove out the spirits with a Word and healed all the sick." (Did you catch that word "All"?) This was to fulfill what was spoken through the prophet Isaiah: 'HE took up our infirmities and bore our diseases.' Matthew is quoting Isaiah 53:4. Matthew says that Jesus healed all, everyone— not just a few or a couple or a small handful. HE healed them all. Pretty powerful stuff and oh so true. This very action of physical healing that was stated in Isaiah is what Matthew is quoting. Since we know Jesus is the same yesterday, today and forever (Hebrews 13:8) and HIS Word is unchangeable and immovable, then yesterday today and forever covers today. Hallelujah!

> **John 10:10b** *"...I have come that they may have life and have it to the full."*

There it is brothers and sisters, straight from the Word of God. Again, this is saying that the enemy is the author of confusion, he deals in conflicts, rebellion and disobedience, stealing, destroying and killing. These are methods the enemy uses to get to our minds, to convince us to focus on the physical, and take our focus off Jesus and the spiritual. Jesus did two things on the cross and at the whipping post: at the whipping post HE received a severe beating thus by HIS stripes we are healed and on the cross, HE suffered and died for our salvation. So we are physically healed and spiritually healed. Thank you, Jesus! When we take a look at John 10:10b, the word "full" also means "overflowing" or "overflows". A life plagued and stricken by illnesses, diseases, and pain contradicts this and other Scriptures. When the doctor says that there is nothing more he can do for you, or there is nothing medical science can do for you, look to Jesus, the Author and perfecter of our lives. He is the supreme Doctor. He's never lost a patient. Look at Matthew 21:20-22. The fig tree has withered. The disciples see this and bring it to Jesus' attention that the fig tree HE cursed has withered so quickly. In verse 21 Jesus says, "Truly I tell you, if you have faith and do not doubt, not only can you do what was done to the fig tree, but also you can say to this mountain, 'Go throw yourself into the sea,' and it will be done. If you believe, you will receive whatever you ask for in prayer." Have faith in God's Word, not doubting what HIS Word says, and ask for in prayer. These are the directions, instructions; our GPS to our healing. Pretty simple, yet we make it so difficult. Believing is seeing; seeing is not believing. We must walk by faith and not by sight, not by how we feel, what things look like, seem to be, or what we hear. Try to rid yourself of the five physical senses and step into the one true spiritual sense, Jesus Christ! Healing is in HIS Word, therefore it is HIS will for you to be healed, made whole, and complete.

Healing is a mindset. Colossians 3:2 says, "Set your minds on things above, not on earthly things." Illness, disease, and sickness are NOT "things above" things! They are earthly! They are certainly NOT found, mentioned or even exist in Heaven or in Jesus. Set your mind on your healing, speaking it out loud, declaring it, praising God the Father, and thanking HIM for your healing. Psalm 22:3 NASB says, "Yet YOU are Holy, O YOU who are enthroned upon the praises of Israel." Psalm 67:3 states, "May the peoples praise YOU God; May all the peoples praise YOU." (Psalm 100 is The "Praise" Psalm. Read it, as it is only five verses, but they are very powerful and encouraging.) As you read this book and allow God to speak to your heart, HE will direct, guide and lead you. If you have any questions, or don't know what to do or what to say…pray, and ask HIM. HE is faithful.

When you look at the Scriptures, the Holy Bible very clearly states that healing is for today!

Galatians 3:29 *"If you belong to Christ, then you are Abraham's seed, and heirs according to the promise."*

Romans 8:10 *"But if Christ is in you, then even though your body is subject to death because of sin, the Spirit gives life because of righteousness."*

2 Corinthians 5:17 *"Therefore, if anyone is in Christ, the new creation has come: The old has gone, the new is here!"*

Ephesians 2:6 *"And God raised us up with Christ and seated us with HIM in the heavenly realms in Christ Jesus."*

These four verses show and say that we are positioned in a very special and specific position in and with Christ. Since Christ never faced any physical attacks such as illness, sickness, disease (and HE encountered and even touched folk who were and never contracted the disease, illness, sickness...), if and when we do, we have the ability and power, Christ's power, to come against the physical attack and receive our healing— doing it, speaking it and receiving it all in the name of Jesus. I really enjoy reading and speaking John 14:12. "Very truly I tell you, whoever believes in ME will do the works I have been doing, and they will do even greater things than these, because I am going to the Father." Even verse 20 tells us "On that day you will realize that I am in MY Father, and you are in ME, and I am in you." That is quite an awesome position to be in and thusly tells us that we have the power and effect to do and say the same as Jesus. On top of all of this blessing and position, we are promised an advocate/comforter, the Holy Spirit. "If you love ME, keep MY commands. And I will ask the Father, and HE will give you another advocate to help you and be with you forever—The Spirit of Truth (the Holy Spirit). The world cannot accept HIM, because it neither sees HIM nor knows HIM. However, you know HIM, for HE lives with you and will be in you" (John 14:15-17). Wow…if that don't light your fire, your wood's wet! Yes, that says that "you know HIM, because HE lives with you and will be with you." That is the voice inside of you, or as the world calls it, your conscience. Ephesians 4:13 says, "until we all reach the unity in the faith and in the knowledge of The Son of God and become mature, attaining to the whole measure of the fullness of Christ." John 6:63 also says, "The Spirit gives life; the flesh counts for nothing. The words I have spoken to you—they are full of the Spirit and life." Life: healthy, abundant, and prosperous life, not disease, sickness, illness, physical ailment or other physical attacks. That is very powerful and it is a spiritual law.

The Bible specifically states that we are Abraham's seed/offspring.

> **Galatians 3:29** *"If you belong to Christ, then you are Abrahams's seed, and heirs according to the promise."*

> **Romans 4:16-17** *"Therefore, the promise comes by faith, so that it may be by grace and may be guaranteed to all Abraham's offspring—not only to those who are of the law but also to those who have the faith of Abraham. He is the father of us all. As it is written, "I have made you a father of many nations" [Genesis 17:5]. He is our father in the sight of God, in whom he believed—the God who*

gives life to the dead and call into being things that were not."

Romans 8:17 *"Now if we are children, then we are heirs—heirs of God and co-heirs with Christ, if indeed we share in HIS sufferings in order that we man also share in HIS Glory."*

Wow, and we haven't even explored The book of Matthew and look what has already been said about us! That is some powerful and very good stuff!

Jesus lived in perfect health, and so should we. Since we live in a fallen and sin-filled world, we (being in this world but not of it) will encounter "things". Even Jesus was tempted by the enemy, but Jesus used the Word of God, responding to each of the enemy's temptations by saying, "It is written..." We must also say and quote Scripture if/when we encounter any type of physical attack and expect the same results Jesus did. Jesus' ministry was three-fold. "Jesus went throughout Galilee, teaching in their synagogues, proclaiming the good news of the kingdom, and healing every disease and sickness among the people" (Matthew 4:23). Teaching, preaching (proclaiming) and healing; there they are, HIS three-pronged ministry. Notice the 3rd mention of HIS ministry— healing! Yes, healing every disease and sickness. Are you getting this yet, is it sinking in?

As I mentioned earlier, there is an account of healing in The book of Luke that none of the other three Gospel writes record and this is found in Luke 13:10-17. Here we read that on the Sabbath (a lot of Jesus' healing came on the Sabbath) Jesus is teaching in the synagogues; "and a woman was there who had been crippled by a spirit for 18 years. She was bent over and could not straighten up at all." Jesus sees her, calls her forward and says to her, "Woman, you are set free from your infirmity." Verse 13 records that HE then puts HIS hands on her, and immediately she straightened up and praised God. Another interesting read on a particular healing account is Luke 18:35-43. When you read this, you will note that the blind man calls out to Jesus. Jesus asks the man what he wants and the man replied out loud, in verse 41, "Lord I want to see." Jesus had the man speak his want out loud, proclaiming it in front of everyone. When the blind man received his sight, immediately, he followed Jesus while praising God. We must praise God right after we ask for, or pray for, our healing. Praising God at that time shows that we have faith in God's Word that we have already received our healing and are thankful. I believe the key is to speak it, to say it out loud, declare it, quote Scripture and what that particular Scripture says about your healing. Our words have power, as I have already mentioned.

"Set a guard over my mouth Lord; keep watch over the door of my lips." (Psalm 141:3).

"Do not let any unwholesome talk come out of your mouths" (Ephesians 4:29).

"The words of the reckless pierce like words, but the tongue of the wise brings healing" (Proverbs 12:18).

"But I tell you that everyone will have to give an account on the day of judgement for every empty word they have spoken" (Matthew 12:36).

Watch what you say and what words come out your mouth. Ask the Lord to put a watch on/over your mouth that nothing unwholesome come out, and if/when it does, that the Holy Spirit nudge you and you are quick to repent of what you said or shouldn't have said. We must; we have to watch what we say and what we speak because our words have power! The very words that we speak, that come out of our mouths, produce a harvest in our heart, whether that harvest be good or bad.

"A good man brings good things out of the good stored up in his heart" (Luke 6:45).

"Above all else, guard your heart, for everything you do flows from it." (Proverbs 4:23).

Jesus connected HIS ability to forgive to HIS ability to heal! Jesus is against sin and HE is against sickness. Sickness is a curse, and Galatians 3:13-14 says, "Christ redeemed us from the curse of the law by becoming a curse for us, for it is written: 'Cursed is everyone who is hung on a pole.'" He redeemed us in order that the blessing given to Abraham might come to the Gentiles through Christ Jesus, so that by faith we might receive the promise of the Spirit.

"How God anointed Jesus of Nazareth with the Holy Spirit and power, and how HE went around doing good and healing all who were under the powers of the devil, because God was with HIM" (Acts 10:38). The Greek word used here for "under the power of" is "katadunasteuo" which literally means to exercise dominion against. It is clear from this text that Jesus was healing all the sick who were "under the power of the devil." Sickness was and still is caused by the enemy himself. (There are a lot of chemicals and things in American foods that are not legal in Europe, and those foods are NOT helping us—they are killing us and causing a lot of diseases and other physical problems.) HE "oppresses" us with sickness. It binds us, keeps us from going out and ministering to folk, serving, and encouraging. God only gives good gifts while the enemy comes to kill, steal, and destroy. Sickness is far from being good. And on top of that, God does not "give" sickness or make us sick to teach us a lesson! That is so ludicrous! Poppycock! Speak life over your body. Speak health to your body. Your words have healing power. Sickness must respond to the power of God, and to the Word of God. That is a spiritual law.

I would like to suggest some things you might say or model. When quoting Scripture, for example, you might say something like, "Lord your Word says…" "Lord, I bind this sickness in the name of Jesus..." "Lord I curse the symptoms and at your Name, the name of Jesus, they must flee my body and healing must come in, nerves, muscles, tendons, blood vessels, arteries…be made hole." You might say something like this, "There is no weapon fashioned against me that shall prosper—You, Lord Jesus, spoke the Word and healed me. I am healed, I receive my healing in your name. Sickness you have no right to be in my body, pain you must leave my body now, in the Mighty name of Jesus! I take authority over you sickness and I command healing to come into my body now! Thank you Lord—I receive my healing, I am cured, pain, symptoms all gone in the name of Jesus. Thank you Lord Jesus, I praise your name. Amen." These are just examples, a sample of a prayer to say, to lift up. I would also suggest you find some Scriptures to write down and keep with you, memorize, carry around with you so you can pull them out and say them. Put them on your bathroom mirror, your refrigerator, your place at work, your locker…etc., and then throughout the day you can see them and say them. Also, you can even pray in the morning, "I thank you Lord that today no weapon fashioned against me shall prosper, therefore no sickness, illness, disease will infiltrate my body..." You are free from sin, sickness, disease, oppression, fear, poverty, lack, want, addiction...God wants you well. "I have come that they may have life and that they may have it more abundantly. (overflowing, to the fullest)" (John 10:10). "However, as it is written: 'What no eye has seen, what no ear has heard, and what no human mind has conceived— the things God has prepared for those who love HIM--'" (1 Corinthians 2:9). "Now to HIM who is able to do immeasurably more than all we ask or imagine (think or dream), according to HIS power that is at work within us" (Ephesians 3:20). "'For I know the plans I have for you,' declares The Lord, 'plans to prosper you and not to harm you, plans to give you hope and a future. Then you will call on ME and come and Pray to ME, and I will listen to you. You will seek ME and find ME when you seek ME with all your heat.'" (Jeremiah 29:11-13). "Dear friend, I pray that you may enjoy good health and that all may go well with you, even as your soul is getting along well." (3 John 1:2). The King James Bible says it this way, "Beloved, I wish above all things that thou mayest prosper and be in health, even as thy soul prospereth." Abundant life cannot be lived, fulfilled, being sick, ill, or diagnosed with some serious disease. Just like our salvation is received by us through HIS Grace, so too is healing...it is a gift from God! Ephesians 2:8-10 says, "For it is by grace you have been saved, through faith—and this is not from yourselves, it is the gift of God—not by works, so that no one can boast. For we are God's handiwork, created in Christ Jesus to do good works, which God prepared in advance for us to do."

The Amplified Bible (AMP) puts it like this: "For it is by grace [God's remarkable compassion and favor drawing you to Christ] that you have been saved [actually delivered from judgement and given eternal life] through faith. And this [salvation] is not of yourselves [not through your own effort], but it is the [underserved, gracious] gift of God; not as a result of [your] works [nor your attempts to keep the Law], so that no one will [be able to] boast or take credit in any way [for his salvation]. For we are HIS workmanship [HIS own master work, a work of art], created in Christ Jesus [reborn from above—spiritually transformed, renewed, ready to be used] for good works, which God prepared [for us] beforehand [taking paths which HE set], so that we would walk in them [living the good life which HE prearranged and made ready for us]." So, based on these and the other Scriptures mentions thus far, if God were to put disease, sickness, and illness on us, it would be hypocritical, wrong and contradictory for Jesus (who only does the will of HIS Father--John 5:19, John 6:38-39, John 12:49 and Deuteronomy 29:29) to heal. Simply put, we must "Trust in the Lord with all your heart and lean not on your own understanding; in all your ways acknowledge HIM, and HE will make your paths straight (direct your steps)" (Proverbs 3:5-6). When we pray we know HE hears us. There are some Scriptures that say this:

"How gracious HE will be when you cry for help! As soon as HE hears, HE will answer you" (Isaiah 30:19b).

"Before they call I will answer; while they are still speaking I will hear" (Isaiah 65:24).

"You will pray to HIM, and HE will hear you, and you will fulfill your vows" (Job 22:27).

"The prayer of a righteous man is powerful and effective" (James 5:16b) The Amplified Bible (AMP) says it this way, "The heartfelt and persistent prayer of a righteous man (believer) can accomplish much [when put into action and make effective by God—it is dynamic and can have tremendous power].

"This is the confidence we have in approaching God: that if we ask anything according to HIS will, HE hears us" (1 John 5:14). And if we know that HE hears us-- whatever we ask—we know that we have what we asked of HIM.

"Therefore I tell you, whatever you ask for in Prayer, believe that you have received it, and it will be yours" (Mark 11:24).

"And I will do whatever you ask in MY name, so that The Son may bring Glory to The Father. You may ask ME for anything in MY name, and I will do it" (John 14:13-14).

"Ask and it will be given you; seek and you will find; knock and the door will be opened to you. For everyone who asks receives; he who seeks finds; and to him who knocks, the door will be opened." (Matthew 7:7-8). Remember, when you ask, you must ask in the will of God, and HIS Word is HIS will. So you must know what HIS Word says about healing and you know by reading HIS Word, studying HIS Word, hearing HIS Word and other ways in which HE will guide and direct you. That is so assuring!

Jesus' healing follows no pattern—you can't figure it out! It's not like a riddle or a puzzle that once you figure out where that piece goes, it fits. It is simply Jesus – the Word in flesh! Search the Word of God for yourselves, study it, see what it says and even ask God for wisdom and knowledge to understand what HIS Word is saying to you. HE will tell you. "But if serving the Lord seems undesirable to you, then choose for yourselves this day whom you will serve, whether the gods your forefathers served beyond the River, or the gods of the Amorites, in whose land you were living. But as for me and my household, we will serve the Lord" (Joshua 24:15). All four Gospels record healing miracles: The book of Matthew the most (27), The book of Mark (21), The book of Luke (24), and The book of John the least (4). We will study the book of Mathew and see what Matthew records about Jesus' healing. "For in Christ all the fullness of the deity lives in bodily form, and you have been given fullness in Christ, who is the head over every power and authority" (Colossians 2:9-10). In the four Gospels, each author has a different account of the same healing, which stands to reason because each writer was a different person. Matthew was a tax collector. Mark, the youngest, was a fisherman. Luke was a doctor/physician and John was a fisherman. As you read and study the healing recorded in the four Gospels you will note the differences of detail. One writer might record the healing with more detail than the other writer. This is evident in the healing of the lady with the issues of blood. Matthew 9:18-26, Mark 5:21-43 and Luke 8:4-56 and John do not record this healing. Matthew records the healing in just 9 verses, Mark in 23 verses and Luke in 17 verses. Mark gives the most detail. Just as with any observation by more than one individual, you are likely to get a little more detail from one than another, but the result will be the same. In this case, as in all the healing cases recorded in Scripture by the four Gospel writers, the result is the same. Healing occurred; no one was turned away or denied, and the healing always took place. Never was one not healed!

We see in many cases of Jesus' healing, that he taught (part of HIS three-fold ministry). "One day as HE was teaching, Pharisees and teachers of the law, who had come from every village of Galilee and from Judea and Jerusalem, were sitting there. And the power of the Lord was present to heal the sick." (Luke 5:17). That is a powerful statement coming from Luke, since Luke was a doctor and yet he says, "And the Power of the Lord was present to heal the sick!" "They went to Capernaum, and when the Sabbath came, Jesus went into the synagogue and began to teach. The people were amazed at HIS Teaching, because HE taught them as one who had authority, not as the teachers of the Law" (Mark 1:21-22). Here, we read that Jesus heals a man with an evil spirit; "Jesus went throughout Galilee, teaching in their synagogues, preaching the good news of the kingdom, and healing every disease and sickness among the people. News about HIM spread all over Syria, and people brought to HIM all who were ill with various diseases, those suffering severe pain, the demon-possessed, those having seizures, and the paralyzed, and HE healed them. Large crowds from Galilee, the Decapolis, Jerusalem, Judea and the region across the Jordan followed HIM." (Matthew 4:23-25). There is no prerequisite, nothing specific needing to be done, no request, HE just healed them, every one of them. In looking at some words and their translations, check out "disease" in Matthew 4:23b. Strong's Concordance has the Greek "malakia" meaning infirmity, debility, bodily weakness, sickness. "Sickness" here in the Greek is "nosos" meaning malady, disease, infirmity, sickness, disability. That seems to me to cover anything that is not healthy, that has a bad or gross physical effect on the body. Plus, the healing is for now, in the physical, with no mention of that healing taking place in Heaven (which we know all physical "junk" is removed when we reach Heaven!) Take a close look at Matthew 4:23-25 again and notice Matthew mentions the inflections and their outcome. Jesus healed everyone. There's no mention of anyone's faith, no mention of anyone asking or seeking HIM, just "people brought to HIM all…" and check out the result, "…and He healed them all." Jesus healed every one of them. Wow, that is pretty awesome!

Just a quick mention of the resurrection of the Dead, we see a parallel in the different stages of death: Jarius' daughter (Matthew 9:18-26) who has been dead for only a little while; the widow's only son from Nain (Luke 7:11-16) who was in a coffin and being carried to be buried, and the death of Lazarus, who had been dead four days (John 11:1-44), were all raised from the dead. "At that very time, Jesus cured many who had diseases, sicknesses and evil spirits, and gave sight to many who were blind. So HE replied to the messengers, 'Go back and report to John what you have seen and heard: The blind receive sight, the lame walk, those who have leprosy are cleansed, the deaf hear, the dead are raised and the good news is proclaimed to the poor. Blessed is anyone who does not stumble on account of ME.'" (Luke 7:21-23). Interesting, and something to chew on! So no matter the stage of death, Jesus brought those dead back to life, and so is the same with healing. It doesn't matter how sick you are, how bad you feel, what the doctor's say, what medication(s) you are on or taking… Jesus is THE healer. Doctor Jesus never lost a patient. Jesus can and will heal the sick, no matter how long one has been sick, no matter the pain, no matter anything, Jesus heals! The same goes with our salvation, too. No matter how long you've sinned, what you have done, how long you've been a sinner... time is nothing to Jesus. HE has no time, HE is the Alpha and the Omega, the beginning and the end. Repent, call on Jesus to save you, heal you, to be your Lord and Savior, and HE will! Ask, Seek and Knock (Matthew 7:7).

Numbers 23:19 says, "God is not a man, that HE should lie, nor a son of a man that HE should change HIS mind. Does HE speak and then not act? Does HE promise and not fulfill?" "For MY thoughts are not your thoughts, neither are your ways MY ways," declares The Lord. "As the heavens are higher than the earth, so are my ways higher than your ways and MY thoughts than your thoughts. So is MY word that goes out from MY mouth: It will not return to me empty, but will accomplish what I desire and achieve the purpose for which I sent it." (Isaiah 55: 8-9,11) "In the beginning was the Word, and the Word was with God, and the Word was God." (John 1:1-2). He was with God in the beginning. When you read these Scriptures, and trust God at HIS Word, than it makes it easier to trust HIM. The enemy has lied to those who are in Christ for so long, using the very Word of God. He has twisted the truth around and then got us to look at the situation, the outcome, and determine that since what we prayed for, wanted and expected did not happen in a certain time frame that it must all be a lie or something else. BUT, since the above Scriptures tell us that God does not lie, HIS Word is truth, the only liar is the enemy. NEVER should a child of God, one who is in Christ, ever believe that it is or was not God's will to heal! People make statements like, "I prayed and asked God to heal _____" or "I trusted God to heal ____ " "…and it didn't work." Based on what evidence: the Word of God or your outcome, your way of figuring out and or thinking the way it should turn out? If it did not turn out the way we wanted,, the way we figured it should even standing on the Word of God, we come to the conclusion that it must be God's will not to save the individual. If we prayed for the salvation of a loved one, for them to claim Jesus as their Lord and Savior and that individual did not accept Jesus as their Lord and Savior, would we conclude that it must not be God's will for that individual to be saved? Of course not, certainly not! Then why do we blame and accuse the Lord that if someone does not get healed it is HIS will not to heal them? It is always God's will to save and to heal. "MY people are destroyed for lack of knowledge" (Hosea 4:6) "The Lord is not slow in keeping HIS promise, as some understand slowness. Instead HE is patient with you, not wanting anyone to perish, but everyone to come to repentance" (2 Peter 3:9). Is it God's fault that not everyone gets saved? Of course not, we have a thing called free will. We choose whether or not we will serve HIM. So we must not blame God or say it is or was HIS will not to heal. There are other factors that are involved— sin, unforgiveness, doubt, not knowing what the Word of God says, speaking the wrong thing— so read the Scriptures, read the Bible, ask God to show you in HIS Word about healing, understanding, receiving your healing; or simply put, what the Word of God says about healing. HE will honor your request, your prayer. HE will show you. "I love those who love ME, and those who seek ME find me" (Proverbs 8:17). "You will seek ME and find ME when you seek ME with all your heart" (Jeremiah 29:13). When you find HIM, you find all the answers to you prayers and HE will speak to you as you speak to HIM. We must also speak HIS Word— declaring out loud what it says about our healing. The enemy is terrified of the Word of God, Jesus, and can not stand against them. "But seek first HIS kingdom and HIS righteousness, and all these things will be given to you as well" (Matthew 6:33). You need to read all of Matthew 6.

Sometimes when you need healing, it might be wise to ask God to show you someone who needs to be healed so you can pray with and for that person to receive their healing. "And MY God will meet all your needs according to the riches of HIS Glory in Christ Jesus" (Philippians 4:19). "Give and it will be given to you. A good measure, pressed down, shaken together and running over, will be poured into your lap" (Luke 6:38). Once again, we see spiritual law put into effect. Ask HIM to supply someone who is in need of healing, go to that person and pray with them. Do not worry about what you will say or how it is you are to pray, HE will direct your words. This can be achieved through prayer, quiet time, reading the Word… and your prayers do not have to be eloquent. HE is concerned with your heart, not your words. And certainly don't forget to praise HIM, thank HIM, and do whatever else you feel like doing at that moment. HE is concerned with your heart, your obedience, and your sincerity towards HIM. He is not impressed with fancy words or long prayers.HE just wants it to be from you,— from your heart. Remember, HE created you in HIS image, and HE knows you. Do not let yourself get caught up in the physical, thinking things like "what will they think?" or "what if it doesn't work, I'll feel silly…" using the five senses. Remember, these are the only way the enemy can come after you and defeat you if you let him. HE cannot defeat the Word of God. Know, expect, trust, and hope through faith that you ARE healed, that your prayers are working, will work and that whether you are praying for your own healing or someone else's based on Scripture, they are healed. Even saying something as simple as, "I am believing for my healing…" verses saying, "I believe that I am healed…" makes a big difference. It may not seem like much but there is power in your words. See yourself as healed; see yourself doing things that you may not have been able to or felt like doing. See yourself feeling better.

These are some Scriptures that you might want to memorize and say: "IN HIM we live and move and have our being" (Acts 17:28). "No, in all these things we are more than conquerors through HIM who loved us" (Romans 8:37). "No weapon forged against you will prevail, and you will refute every tongue that accuses you. This is the heritage of the servants of the Lord, and this is their vindication from ME, declares The Lord" (Isaiah 54:17). "Greater is HE that is in me than he who is in the world" (1 John 4:4). "HE who began a good work in you will carry it on to completion until the day of Christ Jesus" (Philippians 1:6). "If God is for us, who can be against us?" (Romans 8:31). Isaiah 40:25-31 (this read is on you, some good stuff), "I am the Lord, and there is no other; apart from ME there is no God. I will strengthen you" (Isaiah 45:5). "I am God, and there is no other; I am God, and there is none like ME. I make known the end from the beginning" (Isaiah 46:9b-10a). "I, even I, am the Lord, and apart from ME there is no Savior" (Isaiah 43:11). As you continue on reading my book, you will encounter several other Scriptures regarding healing. You can also search the Scriptures for other verses on whatever else you need. Need help finding Scriptures? Search online with Google, or ask a friend who knows and studies the Bible.

You will be surprised how easy and helpful your computer and people will be in you finding what you are looking for.

One thing we need to be careful of in receiving our healing is to try not to understand it, wrap our minds around it, come to a conclusion, or formulate an ending/ how we think it should-will turn out and when. We are to walk by faith and not by sight. We must try to get away from our five senses and not walk by sight, but to do the exact opposite and apply Proverbs 3:5-6, "Trust in the Lord with all your heart and lean not on your own understanding; in all your ways submit to HIM, and HE will make your paths straight (HE will direct your steps)" We MUST let the Holy Spirit guide and direct us. We *must* stand on and trust the Word of God and what it says about healing.

When one looks at and studies all the Scriptures that mention Jesus' healing miracles, there is not pattern, no sequence, no "it works this way". If we could figure it all out, find a certain consistent way that healing worked, then there would be no need for Jesus and no need to trust HIM. The *only* Scriptures where there is any mention of Jesus being only able to heal a few folks is in Mark 6:5, "HE could not do any miracles there, except lay HIS hands on a few sick people and heal them." "And HE did not do many miracles there because of their lack of faith" (Matthew 13:58) Why? Those folks "knew" Jesus in the flesh. They did not acknowledge HIM in the Spirit. They did not have faith in HIM because they questioned who HE was. Matthew 13:54-57 says, "Where did this man get this wisdom and these miraculous powers?" Verse 55 says, "Isn't this the carpenter's son? Isn't his mother's name Mary, and aren't his brothers James, Joseph, Simon and Judas?" Verse 56, "Aren't all his sisters with us? Where then did this man get all these things?" Verse 57 "And they took offense at him." Since they did not put their faith in Jesus as their healer and looked at him as a "normal man", as someone just like them, HE could not do much because they zapped their own healings with their doubt, with their five human senses, especially claiming and saying out loud "who is this man?" Look at what Mark 6:6 says, "HE was amazed at their lack of faith." If you'd like to see the exact opposite of lack of faith, look at Matthew 8:5-13. We will be taking a look at that Scripture in a little bit. We see in the Old Testament that God performed miracles, while Jesus performed miracles in the New Testament. The Old Testament prophesied HIS ability to heal and we see that in Isaiah 35:3-10 and Isaiah 53:4-5. Then in the New Testament, once Jesus became anointed by the Holy Spirit, HE worked HIS divine power to perform healing miracles that defy the laws of nature. (Take a look at John 6:18-21, especially verse 19 and verse 21!) Jesus overcame just about every earthly thing: physical, demonic, weather, nature, material objects, and even death itself, HE overcame! You might ask yourself how do you get that faith in Jesus to perform what HIS Word says? Do what Romans 10:17 says. Consequently, faith comes from hearing the message, and the message is heard through the Word about Christ, ie. The Holy Bible! Pretty simple, yet we can and many times do make it so difficult. Everything Jesus did was perfect, flawless, complete, and it always worked, it never failed, it never did not work! "The Lord said to me, 'You have seen correctly, for I am watching to see that MY Word is fulfilled'" (Jeremiah 1:12). "The one who calls you is faithful, and HE will do it" (1 Thessalonians 5:24). (Now, take another look at Isaiah 55:8-13 and get your socks blessed off!) Unforegiveness, sin, disobedience, pride, worry, and doubt are a few "weapons" that can and will keep your healing from being yours! In some cases, you might just need to fall on your knees and ask, call, or cry for HIS help, telling HIM you can no longer deal with this stuff— this baggage. Just give it to HIM, let HIM deal with it, and free yourself from that junk that has you bound. You do not need to carry this around any longer nor deal with this stuff any longer. "Cast all your anxiety on HIM because HE cares for you" (1 Peter 5:7). "Cast your cares on the Lord and HE will sustain you; HE will never let the righteous be shaken" (Psalm 55:22). We kind of took a little side journey with the above, but I felt it important to add this. Now let's get back to healing and what Scripture says.

"As Scripture says, 'Anyone who believes in HIM will never be put to shame.' For there is no difference between Jew and Gentile—the same Lord is Lord of all and richly blesses all who call on HIM, for, 'Everyone who calls on the name of The Lord will be saved.'" (Romans 10:11-13). Here's a quick translation lesson; "Saved" in the Greek is "sozo" which means to save, same, make whole, heal, be whole, preserve, do well. Deliverance, one's salvation and healing from sickness, are translated from "sozo" (Take another look at James 1:17). "...HIS good, pleasing and perfect will" (Romans 12:2b). Romans 12:1-2 is worth taking a good look at. Jesus mentions that HE only does what the Father tells HIM to do (that is obedience; no questions asked. Jesus just did it and the prime example of HIS obedience is HIS death on the cross, obediently). "For I have come down from Heaven not to do MY will but to do the will of HIM who sent ME" (John 6:38). "Jesus gave them this answer, 'Very truly I tell you, the Son can do nothing by HIMSELF; HE can do only what HE sees HIS

Father doing, because whatever the Father does the Son also does" (John 5:19). "For whoever does the will of MY Father in Heaven is MY brother, and sister and mother" (Matthew 12:50). "'My food,' said Jesus, 'is to do the will of HIM who sent ME and to finish HIS work'" (John 4:34). "By myself I can do nothing; I judge only as I hear, and my judgement is just, for I seek not to please myself but HIM who sent me" (John 5:30). "For I did not speak on my son, but the Father who sent me commanded me to say all that I have spoken" (John 12:49). So to say that it is not always God's will to heal, means that if God put illness on someone, why would one need to pray for Jesus to heal them? We just read Scriptures where basically Jesus is saying that HE only does what the Father tells HIM. So if the Father put that illness on one, there is no way Jesus would heal or could even heal because it would go against the Father. It's contradictory! (Once again take a look at James 1:17, and sickness, illness, disease… these are not "good and perfect gifts".)

Healing Miracles in the Book of Matthew

Let's take a look at the book of Matthew and the recording of healing miracles in this Gospel. The first recorded healing in The book of Matthew is in Matthew 4:23-25); "Jesus went throughout Galilee, teaching in their synagogues, preaching the good news of the kingdom, and healing every disease and sickness among the people. News about HIM spread all over Syria, and people brought to HIM all who were ill with various diseases, those suffering severe pain, the demon-possessed, those having seizures, and the paralyzed, and HE healed them. Large crowds from Galilee, the Decapolis, Jerusalem, Judea and the region across the Jordan followed HIM." Matthew uses some small yet powerful and inclusive words— "every" disease and sickness among the people. He also uses "all" who were inflicted with various diseases, those suffering pain, the demon-possessed, those having seizures, and the paralyzed, AND HE HEALED THEM. You will not find any criteria, special invitations, any requirements, anything…nothing but coming to HIM and receiving from HIM for those needing healing to receive from Jesus their healing. The result, they all received their healing. Matthew presents lists of some pretty sick and physically afflicted folks. There are no red letters, nothing recorded of anyone conversing with Jesus, asking Jesus to heal them and no mention of Jesus touching or saying anything. Everyone just received their healing. This account is also found in Mark 1:35-39 and Luke 4:12-44.

The second healing is in Matthew 8:3b "...immediately he was cured of his leprosy." Beginning with verse 1-3; "When HE came down from the mountainside, large crowds followed HIM. A man with leprosy came and knelt before HIM and said, 'Lord, if you are willing, you can make me clean.' Jesus reached out His Hand and touched the man. 'I am willing,' HE said, 'Be clean.' Immediately he was cured of his leprosy. Here we see the word "immediately" used once, and "clean" used twice, and Jesus touches the man. You will also find this account recorded in Mark 1:40-45 and Luke 5:12-16

The third healing is also found in Matthew 8:5-10, 13: "The faith of the Centurion." "When Jesus had entered Capernaum, a centurion came to HIM, asking for help. 'Lord,' he said, 'my servant lies at home paralyzed and in terrible suffering.' Jesus said to him, 'I will go and heal him.' The centurion replied, 'Lord, I do not deserve to have you come under my roof. But just say the word, and my servant will be healed. For I myself am a man under authority, with soldiers under me. I tell this one, 'Go,' and he goes; and that one, 'Come,' and he comes. I say to my servant, 'Do this,' and he does it.' 1When Jesus heard this, HE was astonished and said to those following HIM, 'I tell you the truth, I have not found anyone in Israel with such great faith.' Then Jesus said to the centurion, 'Go! It will be done just as you believed it would.' And his servant was healed at that very hour." Jesus is asked by the Roman centurion to, "just say the word..." and Jesus comments about the faith of the centurion! The centurion understood authority and the power of words. The centurion had faith in that whatever Jesus said, that is what would happen because when this centurion spoke, people reacted/

responded to his authority. Luke 7:1-10 also records this account.

We continue in Matthew 8:14-17 for healing number four -- "When Jesus came into Peter's house, HE saw Peter's mother-in-law lying in bed with a fever. HE touched her hand and the fever left her, and she got up and began to wait on HIM. When evening came, many who were demon-possessed were brought to HIM, and HE drove out the spirits with a word and healed the sick. This was to fulfill what was spoken through the prophet Isaiah: 'HE took up our infirmities and carried our diseases.'" Jesus here touches Peter's mother-in-law and she is healed, and that evening, many demon-possessed people were brought to Jesus and HE healed them and the sick with a word; HE spoke their healing! Mark and Luke record this healing in Mark 1:29-34 and Luke 4:38-4.

Chapter 8 of Matthew shows us healing number five. In Matthew 8:28-32 Jesus heals two demon-possessed men. "When HE arrived at the other side in the region of the Gadarenes, two demon-possessed men coming from the tombs met HIM. They were so violent that no one could pass that way. 'What do you want with us, Son of God?' they shouted (they recognized who Jesus was, they called HIM "The Son of God"!) 'Have you come here to torture us before the appointed time?' Some distance from them a large herd of pigs was feeding. The demons begged Jesus, 'If you drive us out, send us into the herd of pigs.' HE said to them, 'Go!' So they came out and went into the pigs, and the whole herd rushed down the steep bank into the lake and died in the water." Again, Jesus says to the demons, "Go!" and the demons leave the men and they are healed. Mark 5:1-20 and Luke 8:26-39 also record this healing.

Matthew Chapter 9 has healing number six. "Jesus stepped into a boat, crossed over and came to HIS own town. Some men came brought to HIM a paralytic, lying on a mat. When Jesus saw their faith, HE said to the paralytic, 'Take heart, son; your sins are forgiven.' At this, some of the teachers of the law said to themselves, 'This fellow is blaspheming!' Knowing their thoughts, Jesus said, 'Why do you entertain evil thoughts in your hearts? Which is easier: to say, 'Your sins are forgiven,' or to say, 'Get up and walk? But so that you man know that the Son of Man has authority on earth to forgive sins.' Then HE said to the paralytic, 'Get up, take your mat and go home.' And the man got up and went home. When the crowd saw this, they were filed with awe; and they praised God, who had given such authority to men" (Matthew 9:1-8). Here Jesus speaks saying, "Get up, take your mat and go home!" The man leaves, and there's no record of the man doing anything but leaving, walking home, and carrying the mat that used to carry him! Mark 2:1-12 and Luke 5:17-26 also make mention of this healing.

Healing number seven is also found in Matthew 9:18-26. Here, we read of a ruler whose daughter has just died and a woman who has suffered bleeding for twelve years. They both are seeking healing from the Master. The ruler comes to Jesus, kneels before HIM, and asks Jesus to come touch his daughter who has just died saying, "My daughter has just died. But come and put YOUR hand on her, and she will live." Jesus says nothing but goes with the ruler. "Just then a woman who had been subject to bleeding for twelve years came up behind HIM and touched the edge of HIS cloak. She said to herself, 'If I only touch HIS cloak, I will be healed. Jesus turned and saw her. 'Take heart, daughter,' he said, 'your faith has healed you.' And

the woman was healed from that moment (Immediately)."
In verse 23 we read that Jesus enters the ruler's house with
the flute players and the crowd (noisy, crying, wailing
mourning the "dead" girl) and says, "Go away. The girl is
not dead but asleep." The people laugh at Jesus, but HE
sends the crowd outside (removing all doubters and
faithless folk), takes the girl by the hand and heals her
bringing her back from the dead! So one person comes to
Jesus knowing that if HE touches his dead daughter, HE
will bring his daughter back to life, while another lady
seeks to just touch the hem of HIS garment knowing she
will receive her healing. Both are accomplished! They both
have faith in Jesus, one's faith is in Jesus to raise the dead
and the other is to heal and stop her bleeding, and HE did.
Mark 5:21-43 and Luke 8:40-56 record this miraculous
healing. Healing number eight is in Matthew 9:27-31 in the
telling of "Two Blind Men's Sight Restored". Matthew is
the only writer that records this healing. Verse 27 says that
two blind men followed Jesus and were calling out, "Have
mercy on us, Son of David!" Verse 28 records that Jesus
had gone indoors, the blind men came to HIM and Jesus
asks them, "Do you believe that I am able to do this?" "Yes
Lord," they replied. In verse 29-30, Jesus touches their eyes
and says, "According to your faith let it be done to you;"
and their sight was restored. Jesus asks them for a public
confession and since they believed in Jesus and what HE
could do, they were healed and they received their sight.

Healing number nine is found in Matthew 9:32-34,
"A Mute Demonic Healed" "While they were going out, a
man who was demon-possessed and could not talk was
brought to Jesus. And when the demon was driven out, the
man who had been mute spoke. The crowd was amazed and
said, 'Nothing like this has ever been seen in Israel.' But

the Pharisees said, 'It is by the prince of demons that he drives out demons.' Again, Matthew is the only writer to record this.

Healing number ten is found in Matthew 9:35-38. We see also this is recorded in Mark 6:6-13 and Luke 9:1-6 (particularly in verses 1, 2 and 6). "Jesus went through all the towns and villages, teaching in their synagogues, preaching the good news of the kingdom and healing every disease and sickness (Jesus' three-fold ministry: teaching, preaching and healing). When HE saw the crowds, HE had compassion on them because they were harassed and helpless, like sheep without a shepherd(Also, read John 10:1-18 "The Shepherd and HIS Flock" and Psalm 23:1-6). Then HE said to HIS disciples, 'The harvest is plentiful but the workers are few. Ask the Lord of the harvest therefore, to send out workers into HIS harvest field.'" Here we see two blind men calling out to Jesus by calling HIM "The Son of God!" Jesus asks them if they believe HE can heal them and they say "Yes." Then HE touches their eyes and says that it is according to their faith that they will see. HE also "warns them sternly" not to tell anyone about their healing, but they spread the news about HIM all over the region. Jesus then drives a demon out of a man that was demon-possessed and could not speak. When the demon is driven out of the man, he is also able to speak. In Matthew 10:1 HE called HIS twelve disciples to HIM and gave them authority to drive out evil spirits and heal every disease and sickness. Then, in Matthew 11:4-6 Jesus replied, "Go back and report to John what you hear and see: The blind receive sight, the lame walk, those who have leprosy are cured, the deaf hear, the dead are raised, and the good news is preached to the poor. Blessed is the man who does not fall away on account of ME." These last two scriptures mention

Jesus giving healing authority to HIS disciples and Jesus himself telling a group of John's disciples to report all that they hear and see. Jesus lists all six things that are done: 1. The blind see. 2. The lame walk. 3. Lepers are healed. 4. The deaf hear. 5. The dead are raised. 6. The Good News is preached to the poor.

Healing number eleven is found in Matthew 12:9-14 where Jesus heals a man with a shriveled hand in verse 13; "Then HE said to the man, 'Stretch our your hand.' So he stretched it out and it was completely restored just as sound as the other." Here, Jesus just tells the man what to do and, being obedient, he does what Jesus tells him and his hand is healed. Mark 3:1-6 and Luke 6:6-11 also record this healing.

Healing number twelve is found in Matthew 12:15. "Aware of this, Jesus withdrew from that place. Many followed HIM, and HE healed all their sick." Nothing is mentioned other than HE healed ALL their sick. Mark 3:7-12 and Luke 6:17-19 record this healing.

Healing number thirteen is in Matthew 12:22-23. "Then they brought HIM a demon-possessed man who was blind and mute, and Jesus healed him, so that he could both talk and see. All the people were astonished and said, 'Could this be the Son of David?'" Here, again, nothing is recorded but simply that Jesus heals this man. Mark 3:20-30 and Luke 11:14-23 both mention this and even go a bit deeper. I'll let you read these accounts and conclude for yourself! Healing number fourteen is interesting and not like any others. Matthew 13:53-58, "A Prophet Without Honor." "When Jesus had finished these parables (HE teaches six parables in previous verses in Matthew 13) HE moved on from there. Coming to HIS hometown, HE began teaching the people in their synagogue, and they were amazed. 'Where did this man get this wisdom and these miraculous powers?' they asked. 'Isn't this the carpenter's son? Isn't HIS mother's name Mary, and aren't HIS brothers James, Joseph, Simon and Judas? Aren't all HIS sisters with us? Where then did this man get all these things?' And they took offense at HIM. But Jesus said to them, 'Only in HIS hometown and in HIS own house is a prophet without honor.' And HE did not do many miracles there because of their lack of faith." They had lack of faith in Jesus because they "knew" HIM as a "normal" man just like them so how could HE do/preform these "miracles"? Mark 6:1-6 is the only other write that records this.

Healing number fifteen is recorded in Matthew 14:14 "When Jesus landed and saw a large crowd, HE had compassion on them and healed their sick." Again, in this large crowd that followed Jesus, HE just healed their sick. Luke 9:11 is the only other record of this healing. Like Healing number fifteen, healing number sixteen is in Matthew 14:34-36. "When they had crossed over, they landed at Gennesaret. And when the men of that place recognized Jesus, they sent word to all the surrounding country. People brought all their sick to HIM and begged HIM to let the sick just touch the edge of HIS cloak, and all who touched HIM were healed." Here, the people beg Jesus to let the sick just touch the edge of HIS cloak, and all who touched the edge of Jesus' cloak received their healing! All four Gospel writers record this healing event (along with feeding 5,000 men—many believe that it was upwards to 20,000-30,000 people based on Matthew's record verse 21b besides women and children, the men and their families.)

Mark 6:53-56 is the only other writer that records this healing.

Healing number seventeen is found in Matthew 15:21-28, "The Faith of the Canaanite Woman". "Leaving that place, Jesus withdrew to the region of Tyre and Sidon. A Canaanite woman from that vicinity came to HIM crying out, 'Lord, Son of David, have mercy on me! My daughter is suffering terribly from demon-possession. Jesus did not answer a word. So HIS disciples came to HIM and urged HIM, 'Send her away, for she keeps crying out after us.' HE answered, 'I was sent only to the lost sheep of Israel.' The woman came and knelt before HIM. 'Lord, help me!' she said. HE replied, 'It is not right to take the children's bread and toss it to their dogs.' "Yes Lord,' she said, 'but even the dogs eat the crumbs that fall from their masters' table.' The Jesus answered, 'Woman, you have great faith! Your request is granted.' And her daughter was healed from that very hour." We can certainly see that this woman, a mom, is desperate. Her daughter is suffering from terrible demon-possession. She is, at first, ignored by Jesus and the disciples urged HIM to send her away. She then comes and kneels before Jesus and (I am guessing) cries out for Jesus to help her! Next, Jesus jabs at her, in HIS response that "It is not right to take the children's bread and toss it to their dogs." This does not bother her in the least for her response is, "Yes, Lord, but even the dogs eat the crumbs that fall from their masters' tables." As a result, her daughter was healed from that very hour. The daughter was *healed*, through the "teasing" and her mother's persistence; *not* giving up and having faith in Jesus that HE could and would heal her daughter no matter what and that she was not even supposed to talk to Jesus! And her faith in Jesus and her determination paid off as it always will! She wasn't leaving until she got what she came for! Mark 7:24-30 is the only other writer recording this healing event. (Mark calls this woman a "Syrophoenician Woman", a Greek born in Syrian Phoenicia.)

Healing number eighteen comes in Matthew 15:30-31. "Great crowds came to HIM, bringing the lame, the blind, the crippled, the mute, and many others, and laid them at HIS feet; and HE healed them. The people were amazed when they saw the mute speaking, the crippled made well, the lame walking and the blind seeing. And they praised the God of Israel." There is nothing recorded here that Jesus said anything, there was no asking Jesus to heal anyone, no one touched HIM or HIS garment, they just put their faith in HIM. Only Mark 7:31-37 records this healing event.

Healing nineteen is found in Matthew 17:14-17, "The Healing of a Boy with a Demon" "When they came to the crowd, a man approached Jesus and knelt before HIM. 'Lord, have mercy on my son,' he said. 'He has seizures and is suffering greatly. He often falls into the fire or into the water. I brought him to your disciples, but they could not heal him.' 'O unbelieving and perverse generation,' Jesus replied, 'how long shall I stay with you? How long shall I put up with you? Bring the boy here to me.' Jesus rebuked the demon, and it came out of the boy, and he was healed from that moment." We see here that, for whatever reason not mentioned in this passage, this father brings his son to the disciples who could not heal him. Realizing that Jesus was there, this desperate father goes to Jesus, kneels before Jesus, and tells him exactly what has just happened. There is no record that this father asks Jesus to heal his son, just that he had brought his son to the disciples "but they could not heal him." We see in verse 19 that the disciples privately ask Jesus, "Why couldn't we drive it [the evil spirit] out?" Jesus' response is so powerful and evident today. "Because you have so little faith" (Matthew 17:20). Remember, the disciples were given authority to drive out impure spirits and to heal every disease and sickness (Matthew 10:1, and 8). Their failure to cure this man's son was a result of the disciples forgetting what authority Jesus had given them while focused on the physical. Plus, they had been with Jesus and had seen HIM perform many healing miracles and others. Yet they, being human, forgot what authority they had been given, thus they were unable to drive out the demon from the boy. That's something very common. I would like to address something very powerful that Jesus says in verse 20-21, "Because you have so little faith. I tell you the truth, if you have faith as small as a mustard seed, you can say to this mountain, 'Move from here to there' and it will move. Nothing will be impossible for you." That "faith" is in what Jesus can and will do— what The Bible says HE does. Jesus tells us "I tell you the truth, anyone who has faith in ME will do what I have been doing. He will do greater things than these, because I (Jesus) am going to the Father..." (John 14:12). Wow, what powerful words imputed to you and me— to us! Praise God! Mark 9:14-29 and Luke 9:37-42 also record this healing.

Healing twenty is found in Matthew 19:2. "Large crowds followed HIM, and HE healed them there." Did word of Jesus spread that HE was going to be in this area? Verse 1 says, "HE left Galilee and went into the region of Judea to the other side of the Jordan.") How did all these folks know HE was going to be there? It doesn't matter; the people followed Jesus, and HE healed them. They were plain and simple folk that needed to be healed and had faith in Jesus that HE would and could heal them, and they were healed! Luke 9:54 and John 7:3 mentions this to some extent.

We are now almost done with all the healing Scriptures found in Matthew! There are two more to go over. Healing twenty-one is found in Matthew 20:29-34 "Two Blind Men Receive Sight." "As Jesus and HIS disciples were leaving Jericho, a large crowd followed HIM. [Here we see another reference of a large crowd following HIM. Wouldn't you follow HIM if you had seen and or heard what HE was doing and you needed a healing touch?] Two blind men were sitting by the roadside, and when they heard that Jesus was going by, they shouted, 'Lord, Son of David, have mercy on us!' The crowd rebuked them and told them to be quiet, but they shouted all the louder, 'Lord, Son of David, have mercy on us!' Jesus stopped and called them. 'What do you want ME to do for you?' HE asked. 'Lord,' they answered, 'we want our sight.' Jesus had compassion on them and touched their eyes. Immediately, they received their sight and followed HIM." Wow, lots going on here! Two blind men sitting by the road can't see who is going by, but by the commotion, they sense something "great" is happening. When they hear that it is Jesus, man do they get excited! The shout out for Jesus to have mercy on them. The crowd tells them to be quiet, but they, knowing it was Jesus and could sense a healing miracle about to happen to them, shouted all the louder! This gets Jesus' attention and HE asks them what they want. (Jesus already knew what they wanted and needed, but HE still asks them to go against all adversity and speak it out loud— as if asking them, "how badly do you want to see?" We then see that the "compassion" word is used again. Jesus has compassion on them. touches their eyes, and "immediately" they received their sight and follow Jesus (Add two more to the crowd!) So again we see no pattern, but some repetition, compassion, folk crying out to Jesus for healing, Jesus talking with the folk, asking them what they want HIM to do for them, they saying it out loud, proclaiming what they want, and acknowledging that "Lord, Son of David" is on the scene. And the result; their sight is restored. They are *immediately healed*! I'd like to add that I believe it is safe to say that these two blind men knew that with Jesus on the scene, that HE could and would heal them, by restoring their sight. They had faith in Jesus to do for them what they had probably heard HE had done for others. Interestingly enough, Matthew is the only writer that records two blind men. Mark 10:46-52 and Luke 18:35-43 record this same healing but record only one man. Also noting that in John 9:1-34; this is the only record of this healing where controversy is stirred up when Jesus heals a man born blind.

Healing twenty-two is found in Matthew 21:14. The blind and the lame came to HIM at the temple, and HE healed them. Just healed! Amazing, and praise the Lord, Jehova Rapha, the Lord who heals! Matthew is the only writer that records the healing of the blind and the lame here outside the temple.

I would like to add one more Scripture found in Matthew that does not directly reference healing, but it does do something very powerful and true. In Matthew 21, Jesus curses a fig tree. You can read the entire account Matthew 21:18-22. In verse 19, Jesus says to the fig tree, "May you never bear fruit again!" Matthew records that immediately the tree withered. Now, these next two verses are powerful words from Jesus. "I tell you the truth, if you have faith and do not doubt, not only can you do what was done to the fig tree, but also you can say to this mountain, 'Go, throw yourself into the sea,' and it will be done. If you believe, you will receive whatever you ask for in prayer." This is saying that you can curse symptoms, illness, disease, physical attack, and the source of the physical attack, by following a few simple guidelines:

1. Have faith in the Word of God and what it says.

2. Do not doubt.

3. Get the same results that Jesus got when HE spoke to the fig tree.

4. Tell the "mountain" (whatever is attacking you physically, what you have been diagnosed with…) to "*go*" and it will be done for you.

5. Believe and you will receive whatever you ask for in prayer (your healing!)

Do all of this IN THE NAME OF JESUS! We need to have that childlike faith in Jesus and HIS Word! Hebrews 11:6 says that without faith it is impossible to please GOD! Hosea 4:6a says "MY people are destroyed for lack of knowledge…" We as HIS children, *must know* what *the Word of God* (The BIBLE) says!

Faith in Jesus Christ and the Word of God are essential for healing. Romans 12:3b says "…in accordance with the measure of faith God has given you." We just need to exercise our faith in Jesus Christ and what HIS Word says that HE does when it comes to our healing! God's will is HIS Word! Psalm 56:3b-4 says, "When I am afraid, I will trust in YOU. In God, whose Word I Praise, in God I trust, I will not be afraid." Numbers 23:19 says, "God is not a man the HE should lie, not a son of man, that HE should change HIS mind." 2 Corinthians 1:20 tells us, "For no matter how many promises God has made, they are "Yes" in Christ. And so through HIM the "Amen" is spoken by us to the Glory of God."

So does God ever choose *not* to heal anyone? Nowhere in the Scriptures is that found, except in Matthew 13:53-58, "A Prophet Without Honor". The only folk that Jesus did not heal (notice I said "did not" heal, not could not heal) were the fold that did not seek HIM. You have to know Jesus and know what the Word of God says about healing. Then, having Faith in that is all you need. After reading my book, I hope you can truly and faithfully answer that question with a "NO". You cannot nor will ever be able to find any evidence of that in the Word of God! Does God want everyone to be saved, to come to HIM and proclaim HIM as Lord and Savior of their lives so that He is sitting on the throne of their hearts? Yes! Does everyone get saved? No! Does God want everyone healed? Of course, but does everyone get healed? No! Is it ever God's will not to save or heal anyone? No! Just reading Matthew alone proves that! The real question is are we ready to receive what HE has in store for us? Are we ready to totally surrender our lives to HIM and follow HIS will? Remember, HIS will is HIS Word!

11 More Miracles of Healing

Finally, we see many healing miracles and a few cases of the dead being restored back to life in the book of Acts. This is *after* Jesus had been crucified, buried and raised. The first is in Acts 3:1-8. "One day Peter and John were going up to the temple at the time of prayer—at three in the afternoon. Now a man crippled from birth was being carried to the temple gate called Beautiful, where he was put every day to beg from those going into the temple courts. When he saw Peter and John about to enter, he asked them for money. Peter looked straight at him, as did John. Then Peter said, 'Look at us!' So the man gave them his attention, expecting to get something from them. Then Peter said, 'Silver or gold I do not have, but what I have I give you. In the name of Jesus Christ of Nazareth, walk.' Taking him by the right hand, he helped him up, and instantly the man's feet and ankles became strong. He jumped to his feet and began to walk. Then he went with them into the temple courts, walking and jumping and praising God." What can one say to that other than "Praise God!"

The second healing recorded in the book of Acts is found in Acts 5:12, 15-16. Verse 12 says that the apostles preformed many miraculous signs and wonders among people. Verse 15 says that people brought the sick into the streets and laid them on beds and mats so that at least Peter's shadow might fall on some of them as he passed by. Crowds gathered also from the towns around Jerusalem, bringing their sick and those tormented by evil (unclean) spirits, and all of them were healed. Here we see that Peter's shadow was all that was needed to heal the sick and those tormented by evil spirits.

Acts 8:6-7 records the third healing. When the crowds heard Philip and saw the miraculous signs he did, they all paid close attention to what he said. "With shrieks, evil spirits came out of many, and many paralytics and cripples were healed." Explain this one: "miraculous signs" and when the crowds "heard Philip". They all paid close attention to what he said. Philip must have been saying some pretty powerful things.

Numbers four and five are found in Acts 9:17-18 and 32-42. Acts 9:17-18 records scales falling from Saul's eyes (who was blind for three days). You need to read about Saul in Acts and how he was persecuting Christians. Acts 9:32-42 records Aeneas, a paralytic who had been bedridden for eight years, is spoken to by Peter. "Jesus Christ heals you. Get up and take care of your mat." Immediately Aeneas got up. Verse 35 says that all those who lived in Lydda and Sharon saw him and turned to the Lord. Awesome and true! Verses 32-42 records a dead woman, Dorcas, being raised from the dead. Verses 36-41 read "In Joppa there was a disciple named Tabitha (which, when translated, is Dorcas) who was always doing good and helping the poor. About that time she became sick and died, and her body was washed and place in an upstairs room. Peter sent them all out of the room; then he got down on his knees and prayed. Turning toward the dead woman, he said, 'Tabitha, get up.' She opened her eyes, and seeing Peter she sat up." Verse 42 speaks loudly. It says that this became known all over Joppa, and many people believed in the Lord. Once again, we see healing (this time a person raised from the dead) results in "many people believed in the Lord." We also see that in this case, Peter got down on his knees and prayed. There is no record of Peter's prayer, but he prayed and then spoke! And oh, what results!

Acts 14:3 and verses 7-10 show us healing miracles number six and seven. In Acts 14:3 it is recorded that Paul (who used to be Saul) and Barnabas spent considerable time there, speaking boldly for the Lord, who confirmed the message of his grace by enabling them to do miraculous signs and wonders. There is nothing documented here but miraculous signs and wonders. Let your imagination flow on that one. Verses 8-10 say, "In Lystra there sat a man crippled in his feet, who was lame from birth and had never walked. He listened to Paul as he was speaking. Paul looked directly at him, saw that he had faith to be healed and called out, 'Stand up on your feet!' At that the man jumped up and began to walk." Amazing! Paul recognized (or saw) that he had faith to be healed and tells the man to "stand up on his feet." Without hesitation, without prayer, no shadows, no touching or laying hands on anyone, by just seeing the faith of one wanting to be healed and a command, he was healed! Awesome!

Acts 16:16-18 record healing number eight. We read here that there is a slave girl who has a spirit by which she predicted the future. She followed Paul and the rest of the men around shouting, "These men are servants of the Most High God, who are telling you the way to be saved." As you continue reading, she keeps this up for many days. Paul gets so troubled (fed up!) by this that he turns around and says to the spirit (not the girl, but the spirit), "In the name of Jesus Christ, I command you to come out of her!" At that moment, the spirit left her. This was done by a command, a saying of few words. Again, nothing more, nothing less.

Healing number nine is pretty powerful and uses aprons and handkerchiefs. "God did extraordinary miracles through Paul, so that even handkerchiefs and aprons that had touched him were taken to the sick, and their illnesses were cured and the evil spirits left them" (Acts 19:11-12) What can you say here but "Praise God!"

Healing number ten in Acts is found in Acts 20:9-12. Eutychus is sitting in a third-floor window listening to Paul preach and it is about midnight. He falls asleep, falls out the window and "was picked up dead." Paul goes down stairs to where the man is (instead of having the man brought up stairs to Paul), throws himself on the young man, places his arms around him and says, "Don't be alarmed, he's alive!" Verse 12 says, "The people took the young man home alive and were greatly comforted." And you say…?

Last healing, number eleven, we find in Acts 28:3-9. Paul is gathering brushwood for a fire. As he places the brushwood on the fire, a viper fastens itself on his hand (it bites him). Verse 5 tells us that Paul shakes the snake off into the fire and suffers no ill effects (I encourage you to read all of Acts 28. It is a good read as is all of Acts!) Interestingly enough, the author of Acts is Luke, and remember, Luke is a doctor. Once Paul is bitten, he does not run to Dr. Luke; Paul just shakes off the snake into the fire! Logic might say to run to the doctor, but Paul knew the ultimate doctor, Jesus Christ! Now, I am not advocating anything against doctors, or even saying not to go to doctors. I am just making a statement. Lastly, we see in

Acts 28:8-9 that Publius, the chief official of the island, has his father sick in bed suffering from fever and dysentery. Paul goes in to see him and after praying, places his hand on him and heals him. Verse 9 records, "When this had happened, the rest of the sick on the island came and were cured." When word spreads about people being healed, we see people come from all around to get theirs. More evidence to the healing that is afforded to us *today*! It is not complicated, but the enemy can make it seem that way through lies, deception, lack of knowledge of the Word of God, using our own analytical minds, and using our five physical senses to distract us from focusing on the Word of God and what it says about our healing and other tactics that we give him permission to use against us! The enemy also has us try to figure it out, find a pattern, do this or pray that, pray this way, lay hands on, place a handkerchief (or prayer cloth as sometimes called) or other things that are mentioned in the Bible and mixes them with his lies. Then we begin to focus on logic, not the Word, and thus the tail spin begins, resulting in doubt, wondering, guessing, hoping, supposing, and why-notting! James 1:6-8 But when he asks, he must believe and not doubt, because he who doubts is like a wave of the sea, blown and tossed by the wind. That man should not think he will receive anything from the Lord; he is a double-minded man, unstable in all he does. It is kind of mathematical; 0 x 1,000,000 = 0!

I hope this helps in not only getting a better understanding on what The Bible says about healing, how healing is for us, and receiving what belongs to you and what it cost Jesus (the stripes he bore), but that it has changed and opened your eyes to how available healing is for us *today*! God's richest blessings and HIS favor are on you in Jesus' name. Hebrews 13:8, "Jesus Christ, the same yesterday and today and forever." God's Word in our mouths has the same power and authority as HIS Word in HIS mouth!

Conclusion

Know you are healed. Speak and act as though you are healed, quoting Scriptures out loud that speak of healing. Thank HIM in advance for your healing. Receive your healing knowing that you trust HIM, have faith in HIM and HIS Word that HE already purchased your healing by HIS stripes! Your healing belongs to you, it is yours! See yourself healed. Ignore the five senses and walk in the spiritual realm (walk by faith and not by sight) of your healing. Curse the symptoms and the physical feelings by commanding them in the name of Jesus to get out of your body, and for healing to come in. Do not doubt; rid your mind of any doubt. It is never God's will for you to not be healed and the only folk Jesus did not heal were the ones who did not seek HIM. All who were healed had faith in HIM that HE could and would heal them. HE is the same yesterday, today and forever and is no respecter of persons.

www.ingramcontent.com/pod-product-compliance
Lightning Source LLC
Chambersburg PA
CBHW071637040426
42452CB00009B/1669